THE HUNT

John Kinsella: bibliography

BOOKS

The Frozen Sea (Zeppelin Press, 1983)
The Book of Two Faces (PICA, 1989)
Night Parrots (Fremantle Arts Centre Press, 1989)
Eschatologies (FACP, 1991)
Full Fathom Five (FACP, 1993)
Syzygy (FACP, 1993)
The Silo: A Pastoral Symphony (FACP, 1995; Arc, UK, 1997)
Erratum/ Frame(d) (Folio/FACP, 1995)
The Radnoti Poems (Equipage, UK, 1996)
Anathalamion (Poetical Histories, UK, 1996)
The Undertow: New & Selected Poems (Arc, UK, 1996)
Lightning Tree (FACP, 1996)
Graphology (Equipage, UK, 1997)
Genre (prose fiction, FACP, 1997)
Poems 1980-1994 (FACP, 1997; Bloodaxe Books, 1998)
The Hunt and other poems (FACP/Bloodaxe Books, 1998)

AS EDITOR

The Bird Catcher's Song (Salt, 1992)
A Salt Reader (Folio/Salt, 1995)
Poetry (Chicago) – double issue of Australian poetry
   (with Joseph Parisi, USA, 1996)

JOHN KINSELLA

THE HUNT
& other poems

BLOODAXE BOOKS

Copyright © John Kinsella 1998

ISBN: 1 85224 441 0

First published 1998 by
Bloodaxe Books Ltd,
P.O. Box 1SN,
Newcastle upon Tyne NE99 1SN,

and published simultaneously in Australia
by Fremantle Arts Centre Press.

Bloodaxe Books Ltd acknowledges
the financial assistance of Northern Arts.

Cover printing by J. Thomson Colour Printers Ltd, Glasgow.

Printed in Great Britain by
Cromwell Press Ltd, Trowbridge, Wiltshire.

for HB, TR and GS

Acknowledgements

Some of these poems have been previously published in: *abenteuer & reisen*, *The Adelaide Review*, *Artes*, *Churchill Review*, *Cimarron Review*, *Cordite*, *Heat*, *Imago*, *Interpreter's House*, *Island*, *Kenyon Review*, *Metre*, *The New World Tattoo* (ed. John Hawke, the 1996 Newcastle Poetry Prize Anthology), *Pequod*, *Poetry* (Chicago), *Poetry Daily*, *Poetry London Newsletter*, *Poetry Review*, *Salt*, *Thumbscrew*, *Times Literary Supplement*, *Wasafiri*, *The West Australian* and *Westerly*.

This Bloodaxe edition of *The Hunt and other poems* is longer than the Fremantle Arts Centre Press edition published simultaneously in Australia, and includes several additional recent poems (those on pages 57-62 and 85-93).

The author wishes to acknowledge the support of The Australia Council and the former Prime Minister of Australia, Paul Keating, for a Young Australian Creative Fellowship under the auspices of which many of these poems were written.

Contents

The Well

She'd been fencing it
when the lip gave way
like the flaw re-opening
after corrective surgery. It'd
been bugging her for years,
and even though the kids
were big enough to steer clear
they often had visitors
who wouldn't think twice
about going right to the edge
and peering in. It had gone
salt when she was a kid
and she remembered visiting
her future husband's family
with her parents. The kids
would go down and drop stones
deep into the darkness,
the small implosions of water
returning faintly to the surface.
Now, it was the explosive crack
and sharp cold that caught her.
It rang in her ears as she reached
up towards the noon sun
fixed directly overhead –
a superheated magnet
whose strength belonged
to another reality.
The slippery stone walls
resisted her grip
as if it wasn't seasonal.
And the meniscus of light
deflected her calling
to the point where she
could sense it shimmering
on the metallic surface of the water.
If she knew of liquid nitrogen
a vague image of it may
have anaesthetised her fear.

In the immensity of subterranean time
she noted the eternal falling
of loose earth around the point
of entry. As the flesh
tightened about her bones
she damned the limitations
of the body.

Wild Radishes

Across the dark fields the family is spread
While overhead the sky is haunted,
In the dull light they scour the crop
Never looking up as the day seems to stop.
Wild radishes missed will destroy the yield –
Bills to be paid, deals to be sealed.
But the plover's refusal to lift and drop,

And the absence of crow and parrot talk,
And the immense racket as stalk rubs on stalk,
Register somewhere deep in the soul.
And as the sun begins to uncoil –
The deep green of the wheat uneasy with light –
The golden flowers of wild radishes bite
Just before they are ripped from the soil.

The Tower

When the late-summer sun was fused overhead
The Witnesses arrived at the long southern fence
Parking their car on the road's edge, gingerly climbing
In ankle-length dresses, the deep vermilion
Of their Bibles glowing like stray swamp lights
Caught in the unrehearsed steps of an awkward dance.

The dogs chained beneath the water tank began to dance
Crazily, grinding gravel throats, tugging at rotten posts – overhead
The wooden tower swayed and shimmered while the lights
Of the sun whorled magnetically over the long southern fence,
A twist of wire leaping up and cutting the skin, vermilion
Blood spilling down into the soil, parrots' calls climbing

Indifferently. He walked out to meet them, a piece of climbing
Ivy twisting absently in his hands, watching dragonflies dance
A dazzling techno-mazurka over the exotically vermilion
Waters of the algae-infested fish pond. High overhead
A flock of cockatoos rolled ramshackle towards the fence,
Their pink underbellies counterpointing the Bible's dark lights:

The bodies of their fallen comrades dim spiritless lights,
An outbreak of psittacosis thinning their ranks, the climbing
Mortality rate bringing scientists from both sides of the rabbit-proof fence.
Meeting the Witnesses halfway he noticed the blood and the dance
Of flies about the draining fluid. A dry thunder echoed overhead
Though there wasn't a cloud in the sky. The flies fled the vermilion

Stream as a hand swept down onto them. The vermilion
Covers enhanced the canine vision and the dogs yelped louder, the lights
Of the three figures reflected as one in their tortured eyes. Overhead
The tower expanded with the heat, the temperature climbing
Rapidly, by the minute – its atoms trapped in a dance
Of increasing excitement. As they spoke he glanced at the fence

And noticed that it needed straining, a loose fence
Being the sign that something's amiss, that the vermilion
Gawps of howling dogs are symptomatic of an unsynchronised dance.
Noting the change in his demeanour the Witnesses held the lights
Of their Bibles close to his face, thinking the colour climbing
His skin was a sign of faith. But calling out he motioned overhead.

The dogs broke free and made for the fence as the lights
Were extinguished, their vermilion glows washed by the climbing
Waters, the dance of iron as the tower came crashing from overhead.

Drowning in Wheat

They'd been warned
on every farm
that playing
in the silos
would lead to death.
You sink in wheat.
Slowly. And the more
you struggle the worse it gets.
'You'll see a rat sail past
your face, nimble on its turf,
and then you'll disappear.'
In there, hard work
has no reward.
So it became a kind of test
to see how far they could sink
without needing a rope
to help them out.
But in the midst of play
rituals miss a beat – like both
leaping in to resolve
an argument
as to who'd go first
and forgetting
to attach the rope.
Up to the waist
and afraid to move.
That even a call for help
would see the wheat
trickle down.
The painful consolidation
of time. The grains
in the hourglass
grotesquely swollen.
And that acrid
chemical smell
of treated wheat
coaxing them into
a near-dead sleep.

The Fruits of the Auger

Some of his body fluids
would have made their way
into the paddock – they scooped
the bulk of him from the silo
but it was seed grain
and there was no talk
of compensation
so they removed
the bare minimum.
That it was a bumper
crop was the source
of much laughter
at the pub. Childless
he was considered
more fertile dead than alive.
A couple of regulars
joked about poking his widow
who still laboured
on the property
that claimed his life.
But it was she
more than any
who gloated over
the crop's stunning yield.
In the evening cool
as they emptied
the header bin
into the field bins and trucks
she sat with her back pressed
against the lightning-struck
wandoo, her face wearing
the fixed expression
of a scarecrow
driving unseasonal birds
from the plenty.

Superphosphate

It being a large concern
owned by a city millionaire
who was never there,
everything was bought
in bulk – the feed,
spare parts for the plant,
fencing gear, fertiliser.
The 'super shed'
took enough to topdress
thirty thousand acres.
White mountains
climbed towards
the corrugations
of the roof, moisture
had gone and left
a greyish crust on the surface.
Despite skin burns
from the chemicals
workers' kids would spend
their holidays burrowing
into the hard snow.
'Didn't I tell you to keep
out of it, you little bastards!
It'll come down on you
and that'll be an end of it!'
the boss would yell
as he walked by,
forgetting about them
before they were out of sight.
But despite minor cave-ins
they survived. And one day
they found a mouse nest
near the back of the shed.
They excavated a short way
below the surface and found
a crystallised family,
the snow forming a chrysalis
for the bodies'
metamorphosis.

Hessian

As the children swaddle the old dog's corpse in hessian
Their grandmother recalls seeing her parents
Preparing her stillborn sister for a bush grave.
She says she watched from behind the curtain
As they placed a small bundle wrapped
In linen inside a hessian sack – the red stamp

Of ASW wheat glowing like the stamp
Of death. She had seen and touched that hessian
Earlier in the day when it had wrapped
The jointed wooden doll that her parents
Won in the town raffle – hiding it behind the curtain
Until her birthday. She would take it to the grave.

As they lower the bier into the grave
She reaches out – they hesitate while she examines the stamp
And touches the heavy-fibred cloth, a dark curtain
Of mist falling from her mouth onto the hessian
Gleaming with black frost. Their parents
Would be angry with them for being unwrapped

And out in flu-weather, for being wrapped
In the macabre evocations of the grave
Their grandmother brought down from her parents,
When time and time again they had tried to stamp
Out such superstition, cure her fetish for hessian
And the spiritualism of the curtain.

But all children know the truth of the curtain
And cannot avoid being wrapped
In thoughts of the otherworld. And hessian
Is omnipresent out there on the farm, and the grave
Is a common sight, headstones bearing the stamp
Of the family, the names of the parents of parents:

Set along roadsides and in paddocks, parents
Lie beside their children's homes, a brick curtain
Dividing each transit zone, the ASW stamp
Long eroded, a chemical residue wrapped
In dirt – the dirt they examine with grave
Expressions when the rains don't come – seed still in hessian.

As they move quietly back inside to be wrapped
In the Wonderheat's generous warmth, talk of the grave
Is abandoned – spread over the paddocks like hessian.

Dogs

The pack moves through the lower paddock
Late at night, the daylight moon
Will reveal the work of their 'black dawn',
The blood high on their throats, the cur-ish
Whimper as the weaker dogs lick
The death-fluids from their matted fur
So that, dispersed among their many homes,
Their other life might be hidden – head down
And a slow movement of the tail
Suggesting compliance, the dark doings
Quickly forgotten. But collectively
They respond to the leader's howling,
And jump fences, whine and work at chains,
Prick their ears up and leave their bedding.
The sheep on remote farms sense their coming.
The leader – no yellow cur with distant eyes
But the local magistrate's pedigree Alsatian –
Draws his nocturnal army towards relief;
And as the pack of assorted breeds plunges
Into the frenzy, the carnage of the moment
Becomes complete: the sheep corpses
Like beacons in the haunting darkness,
Driving home the impotence of their conquest.

Death of a Roo Dog

One of the dogs chased a boomer
right down from the forest's edge
to the house dam where it plunged
into the ochre waters up to its chest.
Before I could grab the mad dog's collar
it launched itself straight in after
a roo that I'd swear stood higher
than me by a head. And that wily
creature, its tail anchored
in the muddy bed, levered
its toenails into position
and ripped open my best dog
from top to bottom, and then
pressed down until the remaining
life was thrashed into darkening
waters. I was too stung to shoot
as that monster roo lurched
onto the banks, glutted
with battle, eyeing me defiantly,
its back turned on this Pyrrhic
naval victory.

Emu Hunt

They'd drive them down this stretch of track
At breakneck speed, and then two guys
Hiding behind those thick-set wandoo trees
Would snap the rope tight at breast height
And toss them arse-up, leave them sprawling
Bulbous-eyed, with claws grasping at thin air,
Necks twitching like headless snakes
Waiting for the calm of sunset, tarantismic
Feathers fanning the ground like chopper blades
Skewed off-centre, the staccato of bullets
Sprayed from rapid-fire semi-automatics,
Reverberating through the forest canopy,
Meat ants driving hastily towards the corpses.

Echidna

(for Jacques Derrida)

Rhythmically burrowing up on the toproad
in the graded remainders, the swampy contours
that look good for digging, that you'd
like to get amongst and smell –
those substrata, more than dirt and roots,
rhizomic agendas of the feeble-eyed,
uttering up refrains from where
compactness and density
are demarcation and territory,
where decaying mallee root
or corpse of storm-felled wandoo
tan the leathery bag of muscled fluid,
the flow of ants as white as Moby Dick,
as determined against the pulpy hull of trees
as against the gridded surface. Down where
the highway is sensed in the movement of sand-
particles, the *hérisson* – *istrice* in Italian,
in English, hedgehog – excavates
determinedly. At risk, this bristling heart
litters the roads with dedication,
symbols of the national psyche
left to bloat in the sun's blistering
prosody: *inseparation* that mimes
mechanics on the surface: *<by heart>*,
that without footnotes is still recognised
as the source of all under-movings.
I consider as memory tracking an echidna
with a farmer in jam tree country –
locating the spirit of place,
as if its being curled in a tree hollow
might validate the vast spread
of open tillage – but struck
by a kind of amnesia we wandered
in a circle tight as a fist, exhuming
the deeply choric question of rendering
our meanderings into prose,

into idle chatter to accompany
a few beers in the pub that night;
the portfolio of our imagined data
presented with detachment
as the slow-moving underminer
of our confident lyrical selves
fed ravenously,
deep in the heart
of the forest.

The Disappearing

The freshwater stream
kept that dam full
even during drought.
It had never gone dry.
And at the peak
of the drought – the heat
as heavy as thunder-heads –
he wandered down
along the line of withered
redgums onto the watershed
and into the greyish
cool waters. That he was
a farm boy and knew better,
that their backs were
turned just for a minute,
didn't make him reappear.
It was a gesture as complete
as the absence of rain.
It was a phenomenon
as strange as the heat-warped
fence-posts that stood
at about his height
and betrayed
a child's movements.

Dam and Globe of Death

On the old Suzuki 100 –
that black bike
that weighed
too much
for its
engine capacity –
a cousin rode
the dam walls
like the globe of death,
horizontal over the muddy
waters at the height of summer
with a meningitis alert
ringing in his ears –
waterbirds
retreating over
the wind-burnt fields,
the sheep running
as if the world
were turning
beneath their hooves.
Centrifugally
he spun around
the seasonal watermarks,
working his way
up the wall
like an illusion,
a mirage driven
by machinery
imported
by a mountebank
who'd end up
with mud on his face
and be driven
from the land.

Fences

1

The pasture's greener over there,
I don't think they're in need of repair.

2

The neighbour's sheep are in our field,
It's time those bloody gaps were sealed!

A Black Moon

We've got to go against the grain
they told the group, a bunch
of middle-aged city-folk
who'd come down for a weekend's
relating to the bush.
That their hosts had only
been currency in those parts
for a couple of months themselves
wasn't mentioned. *Tonight*
we'll confront our fears,
do what we'd never do
by ourselves. We'll go out
into the wastes with nothing
but a torch, and then cut the light.
We'll let our fear fill us
until we burst, and then
feel freedom take its place
as it spills and vanishes
like Indian ink in darkness.
Some were hesitant
but the group's energy
carried them out into the
wide open spaces – hand in hand,
the blind leading the blind.
Sitting down beneath a black moon,
they told stories, muttered prayers,
felt heavy with the silence
that clamoured about bones,
replaced flesh. *Freedom* surged
as fear fled like shadows
under a midday sun.
A rumbling was heard in the distance.
They remained calm. It grew closer.
A pinpoint of light appeared
wavering crazily.
And then, as rifle shots
cracked and spat at fear,
they rose up as one,

their single torch a spark
leaping between unstable poles.
At least, that's how the boys
tell the story on Friday nights:
'Just to give them a fright,
you know, hear them say,
Don't shoot! Don't shoot!
before retreating out of the night.'

A Lynching Under the Southern Cross

A few years back there was an attempted
lynching beneath the Southern Cross windmill
on the scrub side of the 'new' dam.
It was at sunrise and three ute-loads
of revellers from the Bachelors' and Spinsters' Ball
saluted the occasion as the windmill barely
turned in the light summer breeze
that came whispering over the rust-red
stubble. In double-breasted suits
and short black dresses, toasts were drunk
as the long figure of a partygoer
grew longer, head shrouded in
a hessian bag, the thin noose
snarling about the flesh of his neck.
'That'll teach you for gettin' into
black meat, you dirty bastard!'
someone yelled as the feet twitched.
'Them students that come up
to work on the bins are perverts!'
'That'll teach the bastard for telling me
I've got wet loads and for docking me
every time I drive in. Hasn't got
much to say now, has he?' Cans of beer,
warm and shaken, fizzed into the day.
Stunted eucalypts in the 'scrub'
knotted as the blue of the sky
formed a negative impression
of the suffocating man.
The rope, fraying with expectation,
snapped with his weight.
He was not, as was later said,
cut down by the boyfriend
of the *belle of the ball* – she'd been pissed
rotten in the back of a ute, her
boyfriend's best mate feeling
her up while the hanged man
struggled. No, he just fell in a heap
and they left him there. After a while

the condemned man picked himself up
and removed the hessian sack,
his swollen eyes gradually
focusing on a pair of crows
pacing about the empties,
eyeing him suspiciously.

The Hunt

(for Les Murray)

A bounty of 'fame throughout the district and no
chores for a week' was placed on The Tiger by my
                Uncle. We'd all seen it
                plenty of times over
the years – a huge beast that came down from the Top Bush
and raided the chicken coop, took the guinea fowl,
                and slaughtered pets. It was
a true feral, begotten by ferals. It was,

in a sense, a species entire in itself.
Those many sightings over the years of a 'large
                predator' we put down
                to The Tiger. It seemed
like a joke of nature – green-grey fur with musty
yellow waves running like stripes down its flanks, massive
                jaw with steel teeth that shone
as it snarled in a spotlight before vanishing

into the bush. For two years it had been hunted –
even the local pro fox shooter couldn't bring
                home its scalp. One winter
                holidays my cousin
and I packed our tent and kit, shouldered arms and crossed
into the scrub. Deep into the dark forbidding
                foliage we plunged. We struck
                camp close to the centre
of the island of wandoo and mallee, a large

copse surrounded by florescent green crops of wheat.
At dusk we shot three grey rabbits as they emerged
                from their warrens. It was
                quick and nothing was said.
Placing them in a damp hessian sack we spent hours
traipsing through the bush by torchlight, dragging the sack
                behind us. The scent spread,
                we emptied the corpses
on a patch of open ground and set to digging

31

hollows and laying traps – fierce iron jaws decayed
by rust, straining beneath sand-covered newspaper
              disguising the ambush.
              We took turns in laying
them, one holding the torch, the other spiking chains
into dirt, bracing springs with a boot. The traps ringed
              the offering. Rubbing
the ground with a corpse we masked our sharp scent before

casting it back on the pile. The cold bit at our
bones. Finished, we didn't linger – a strange fear took
              hold of us and something
              nudged its way under our
confidence. We returned to the campsite. Morning
was bitter – tamarisks were heavy with frost, sheathed
              with rapiers of ice.
              We struggled with a fire,
ate by the smouldering, eye-stinging hearth. Rifles

in hand we made our way to the place. *The Altar
of the Dead* one of us muttered without humour.
              The Tiger was there. Dead –
              frozen solid. The stripes
on its flanks blurred by the dark matting of fur. Three
of the traps had snatched its limbs; the others had been
              triggered and lay beaten
nearby. The Tiger had chewed off its trapped forepaw

which lay half-digested in the trap's maw, back legs
stretched as if by some medieval torturing
              device. The carcasses
              of the rabbits had not
been touched. We buried them with The Tiger; buried
the traps, deep. We packed our gear and went home, telling
              Uncle that The Tiger
              would never be caught, that
it was a creature not of this world – a bitter
cold had struck our bones, fire bringing no relief.

Death of an Infant

The town was divided over the death of O'Henry's youngest.
    There were plenty of us who'd lost children at birth or as infants.
But old man Pierce who'd been returning the long-necked auger
    He'd hired from O'Henry saw him at the back door threatening
To break it down with an axe if his missus didn't let him in.
    Pierce, knowing his neighbour's weakness for strong liquor
And wary of his explosive temper, dropped the auger so its snout
    Crashed into the dirt, and set off home for his shotgun.
A superstitious fellow, he noticed as he tore out of the house paddock
    A chicken with its neck stretched hanging from an apple tree
And horseshoes suspended upside down from the fence
    So the luck had run down into the reddish-brown earth.
When he got back he found the back door in splinters.
    O'Henry was nowhere to be seen. He called out and Mrs O'Henry
Came to the door in tears, crying out that a bitter draught
    Had reached up from the fetid ground down by the creek
        And drawn the life from her baby.

A Tale from Sand-Plain Country

Where the coast meets the sea
Four hundred kilometres north
Wheatfields go right up to the dunes
Which shift with winds so strong
They bend trees. Postcards are sold.
Once the Devil played cards
In a small stone pub
And his opponents
Noting his luck change
As the stakes got high
Checked to see if he'd been
Marking cards under the table.
As plain as day they'd seen
His cloven feet and had as one
Watched as he passed
Directly through the wall,
Scorching the dry fields
As if a flame had been caught by the wind
And dragged away from the coast
Towards the dark centre
Of the continent.
They marked the charred patch
Where he'd passed through the stone.
At the Cathedral in Aachen
The same Devil left his finger
Behind in the mouth of a lion,
Though this was some time before.
Stroking the bronze wolf for luck
You might wonder if time
And place were relevant to him.
The story in this case
Goes something along
The lines of the following:
That in order to finish the Cathedral
When times were hard
The people of Aachen promised
The first soul to enter the building
Upon completion to the Devil.

When time for payment came
They hesitated. Of course,
No one would enter
This Byzantine wonder –
Seat of Charlemagne – out of fear
Theirs would be the soul
The Devil took as his due.
So a wolf was forced through the doors.
Furious, the Devil shook the building
And storming out, slammed the doors,
His finger catching
In the lion's-mouth handle
As it ripped shut. This story
Is of particular relevance
As the family who owns that farm
Touching the coast
Are of German extraction,
On the maternal side. Otherwise
It's fifth-generation Irish.
The old man says they only
Got the land because it was sold
For a song – only good for a few sheep.
It wasn't until much later
That farming on sand-plain country
Was pioneered. And while English settlers
Had all the rich land south
He points out that
Much of it has turned salt.
On the seaside of the dunes
You wouldn't know
That things could grow
Only a few hundred metres away.
It is as barren as a beach can be
And there are no reefs or sandbars
To protect the shore
From a constant barrage
Of black waves. Savage rips
Mean that visitors
Are warned not to bathe.

The Hastings Fence-Post Digger

Always innovating, his brother
Invented a fence-post digger.
A chip off the old block
It was a straightforward
Kind of device – you screwed
It into the dirt and pulled
Out the compacted earth
Just like coring an apple.
Up until then it had been
Backbreaking work
With long-handled shovels.
What of it that some company
In the city had been marketing
A similar device for years?
His brother died none the wiser,
Satisfied that he'd
Made his contribution.
That he'd be remembered forever
As the inventor
Of the Hastings Fence-Post Digger.

The Publican

When the ol' man died
she went straight to town
and drank herself silly.
She said that if it was okay
for a bloke to drown his sorrows
when his missus left him
then why not her? If you
don't get to the corpse
we'll smell it from here –
we can't be more than twenty
miles from your place, they said.
I'm going to sell it and the dirt
it's lying on and buy this pub
and that'll shut your mouths.
Which she did. And her
regular donations to CWA
and Lions Club and the free use
of her function rooms keep
the gentry happy. Though
the boys in the bar call her Mum
and smack her bum, a kind
of incest that has them
joking over her short skirts
and stockings but all hoping
to lie in her arms
when no one's looking.
One day she drank with a stranger
and took him to her room.
He drank there for two days after
and getting loud she asked
him to leave. Take what you want
and then dump me? he mocked.
The boys who hated him
warmed to his sarcasm.
Each bite was a bite they'd take
for their confused emotions.
Nipples like .303s he yelled.
Even the skimpies laughed.

She crumbled a pretzel
between thumb and finger,
careful to disguise the laughter
fermenting deep inside her.

Relics
(for Tom Griffiths)

1 *The Anthropologist*

Because he'd drink with the locals
And would have a go at chucking a spear
He thought it okay to take a few relics
Back to the city. After all, most of them
Were found objects, like pieces of flint
That had been chipped into sharp tips,
Or larger chunks that might have been
Used for shaping tools. It wasn't as if
They were mere souvenirs, each had
A special sentimental value. Though
Where he'd store his private collection
When he went to New Guinea to record
Cargo Cult tendencies in mountain
Communities he wasn't so sure.

2 *Rock Paintings*

Slim went straight up there as soon
As he heard and took to them with a hammer.
By the time we got there he'd obliterated
All trace of them. And even then he said
He'd a good mind to set a stick of gelignite
And blow the whole lot to kingdom come.
Apparently his sister had shot off
A whole roll of film on making the discovery.
He demanded she hand it over
And when her husband stepped in
And told Slim to take it easy, Slim
Decked him right where he stood. He took
The film and exposed it to the midday sun.
The boys needled him a bit at the pub
About skeletons in the closet but he'd
Got his sense of humour back and took
It pretty well. When a black guy came in

To get a takeaway Slim put his arm around
His shoulder and treated him like some
Long lost friend. Shouting him a game
Of pool, buying him a couple of drinks.

Ne Plus Ultra

For twenty years
he'd been rebuilding
that van from the chassis
up.
   A grand Sand Man
from the mid-seventies
when sin-bins were
the coolest thing on the street.
It's got a three five one
port & polished under the bonnet,
twelve-inch mags and a split diff.
He'd been working the interior
for five years – crushed velour,
portholes, designs straight
from a book of Odin's tattoos
he sprayed himself.
            Every night –
(home from the meatworks) – under spotlights
he'd push his masterpiece a stroke
closer to completion. A few cans
and a couple of bongs and into it.
It was his fortieth birthday.
His parents were old.
The shed he lived and worked in
was out back, a short way
down the paddock. A bull terrier
with a spiked collar chewed
on beer cans outside
in the reddish dirt.
          A couple
of the blokes brought girlfriends
but women felt uncomfortable
around him.
       Looks at you
sort of cockeyed, you know
what I mean? The blokes would
joke it was the metal plate
in his head. *Kicked by a cow*
at the meatworks when he was a kid.

Never complained, got a
job-for-life, or at least
until they close down.
Most of the cattle are trucked
to the port now.
                    Being strangers
we asked about the name
painted in black Gothic script
on each side of the van: **ne plus ultra**.
Well, that's what some quack
said to him when he spieled
on about his van. Nobody knows
what it means. But Matt reckons
it'll help him pull the chicks
when he finally
                    hits the streets.

Reticulating the Avocados

Having sold off the top paddocks to finance
The overdraft, they looked to diversify.
The market price high, they took a chance

On avocados, being the first to defy
The recommended climatic conditions,
To plant despite the frosts and dry

Biting heat of the district – the frisson
Of succeeding against the odds
Driving them on despite derision

From locals who gave sarcastic nods
To each other in the town's main street
No doubt secretly afraid that the gods

Might in their fickleness choose to greet
The scheme with favourable reports
And bring avocados to their world of wheat

And sheep, nurture an enclave of foreign fruits.
But a dry place with a sun that burns
Even the toughest plants to the roots

Does not lend itself to altruistic turns
And will ignore even the offerings
Of the most obsessive Dionysians.

So after preparing the soil to take each seedling
They created a second atmosphere
Beneath a field of shadecloth, unwinding

Rolls of plastic piping, hoping to auger
Water down from the dam, to feed
It through the network, to steer

Its life-giving properties to the orchard.
But despite the influence of gravity
The water refused to be drawn, the red

Soil that tainted the dams of the valley,
Weighed heavy in the pipes. Attaching
A pump they forced the slurry

Down onto the field, slowly flooding
The plot like the fertile plains
Of an alluvial delta. With nurturing

The trees grew slowly while the grains
Were harvested. Frosts and blight
Bit into their flesh and the telltale stains

Of fungus appeared on their skins. Despite
These setbacks most of them bore
Fruit within four years. At first, a light

Crop, but then each year brought more.
The town talked about the prices they'd charge
For avocados in the fruit and veg store.

Gradually others saw the advantage
And began to plant using the same scheme.
Avocados became all the rage.

The Great Drought ended the dream.
The red water set solid in the pipes,
Arteriosclerosis choking the system.

The Faulty Bolt Action

The cross-lock-slip-up on the rickety gate
lets flow the flock into the plump ears
of wheat, the stock blowing up and dropping
like dead weights, conversely the faulty
bolt action of the rimfire twenty-two
lets the target slip away into the scrub
or below the earth when the spell
of the halogen spotlight is broken.
Those scorned for failing to slip
the firing pin into place, to brace
the slug within its rifled chamber,
should be praised. Like my brother
who perfected the art of ejecting
every bullet grabbed from the falsely
artistic lines of the curving magazine
at the vital moment. As an adult
his sight is not obscured like some,
who track their way towards
the evening sky with a compass
marked in blood. The rusty actions
of gates a contradiction that gnaws,
a compulsive need to check
the task, to ensure they've done
exactly what it is their
conscience dictates.

Jackknife

The back end catching up
& skewing shockingly
across the hitching pin,
jagging sideways and cracking
the spine of the truck,
trailer arse-up & the driver
shot through the windscreen
over the bullbar, his load
of sheep ground into a rough
slurry, minced through the grilles,
the asphalt a rink filled
with a greasy slick of blood
on which tailing vehicles
slide into the grotesque
haute couture of metal
and Pure New Wool – a pile-up
on the Interstate Highway,
an epistemological
wreckage.

Ultralight P(r)oem

Assembled in a jiffy the ultralight clamours upwards with a persistent nervy buzz. Sheep stampede with its approach, neighbours eye their shotguns. With your average Cessna or larger metal bird there is a sense of distance, or immutability between earth and sky. What they see, if anything, from up there can't quite be real because they have transgressed the laws of nature and therefore can only experience what they see in a removed, displaced, almost surreal way. But the ultralight is different. It's like giving wings to the human. Nothing so graceful as bird wings, but rather insect wings – more frenetic and ground-orientated than the metaphorical bird. There's a touch of the dragonfly about it, but none of the meditativeness evoked by the dragonfly. More like an irritating parasite – the mosquito most readily comes to mind. But on a restless summer's evening its retreat over the low hills is part of the relief you look for at the end of a long and trying day.

The A-Type Wheat Bin

1 *dreadnought*

structuralist and economic
this dreadnought glares brighter
than the tinder-stark fields
that frame it, held in dry dock
by a bed of asphalt and a minefield
of firebans, protector
of the shire's wealth,
its walls thick enough
to stave off even the most
concerted attack,
though deep within
the yellow stacks
rodents run like rust

2 *fumigation*

the pesties move in
and bomb the stacks,
the outer façade
impervious,
unseen the writhing
rats and mice
as outside
only birds
break the silence

3 *roof space*

the de rigueur rusty galvanised tank
that, feeding off the vast armour-plating
of the A-type wheat bin, sits unashamedly
in contrast: the motto reading, where
it's dry for most of the year,
'never waste roof space'.

4 *sampling hut*

perched high above
the lines of trucks
with their tarped and bulging loads
of freshly harvested grain
the metal gantries control the bin

as if extensions of the stand
samplers send metal spears
deep into the loads
to extract a vein
of the paddock's blood

the analysis of moisture and protein content,
the observation of foreign bodies,
the scrutinising for moulds and rusts,
blights and cracking,
the weighing up

the signature that sees the truck
moving down to the weighbridge,
or heading back to an angry farmer
whose harvest moves rapidly
towards disaster

5 *weighbridge*

the subtraction of gross and net
will leave a truck idling like
the trepidation of figures
never calculated: an accountant's
persistent anxiety

6 *grid*

grain dust hovering
over the grid might sense
even the briefest spark
from an errant cigarette,
its raging allergy
triggered, sending
explosive shocks
through the body's
cavity

in this way
entire harbours
in distant ports
have been lost

7 *stack*

like the smallest particles
swollen to macro-proportions
grain spills from the conveyor
and spreads over the floor
of the A-type, gradually proving
like bread against tin,
rising to a peak
in dusty
fetid air

8 *view from the tower*

high up there the vista
turns like a cyclorama
as machinery
intensifies the silence
of space

all is compressed
into the flat disc
of sight: ripples and rises
ironed into tawny fields,
whorls of unharvested stalks
tidal and leaning
in and out,
against the lines
of currents stretching
through beheaded
flatlands, stubble
endlessly red, spotted gums
tortured beneath
the stringent blue
of the sky

9 *quarters*

six blokes crammed
into a fibro hut on stilts
with the pommy
finding a dugite
in his kit
still writhing
despite the sun
having already set

Wrapping the Hay

The hay has just been stacked
in neat yellow bricks like some complex
puzzle that needs to be solved.

The sheds full, it sits alone out there
in the stark yellow paddock – pathetic edifice
waiting to be torched or blown away.

But it's got Escher written all over it
so there's a sense of the infinite.
Though early summer storms

can be pretty savage around here.
Lightning-struck trees along the roadsides
are testament to this. Dad reckons

we'd better get straight to it. Covering
the stack with blue plastic sheeting
and staking it deep in the ground.

School's just finished and next
year it'll be university in the city.
Art history. None of this landscape

stuff – give me Jeff Koons fucking
Cicciolina, those fleshy cybernauts
without a field or ear of wheat

in sight. So it's hard to get motivated
and Dad tells me I'm not too big
for a clip under the ear. I wonder

if he's joking but get out there
with my brothers and get stuck into it.
I tell them about *Far from*

the Madding Crowd and work up a sweat
thinking about Cicciolina. And how stylish
it would be to have a film version

with Koons instead of Alan Bates.
But keeping Julie Christie as
Bathsheba Everdene. Gross!

The blue plastic flaps viciously
as the wind lifts. It cracks in our faces.
It catches my youngest brother

and slices his cheek. The blood
spray-paints the hay. He keeps
at it, swearing at the top of his voice.

Lightning highlights the installation
and for a dreadful moment
we seem to be furiously adrift

in the vast ocean of the paddock.
Over the hills where the storm's dark eye
dilates. The rain drives hard

and I forget about everything. Finally
the hay is wrapped. Christo appears
in my head and I keep him there.

On the Random Distribution of King Parrots

(for Harold Bloom)

Clustered in a mallee ash, swinging upside down
and exposing the red heart of confidence, these
    Blue Mountain king parrots
behave according to their listing in *Slater's*
Australian Field Guide. Surveying the apparent
    wealth of wet sclerophyll
    forest, they remain high
in the grey deadwood. Indigenous and content,
even the threat of diminishing habitat

fails to dislodge them. Once, I saw a pair of king
parrots where they should not have been. It was between
    Wandering and Williams.
They were feeding on a corrugated gravel
road with a small flock of regent parrots – *smokies*
    as we call them back home.
    It was sultry weather
and the moisture suggested the colours of each

species ran like waterpaint over the yellow
grain spilled from the backs of loosely tarped trucks. Stephen
    said he had seen a few
around over the years. The farmer at Happy
Valley reckoned they'd have escaped from aviaries.
    Driving home on the same
    road I found the remnants
of a flock of *smokies*, hit en masse by a fast-

travelling vehicle. In the centre, one orange
heart was exposed, its partner nowhere to be seen.
    The landscape I come from
is often perceived as *surreal*: but it's the sound
of a chainsaw as it tears into mallee ash,
    an orange symphony
    of king parrots straining
to make itself heard high overhead, that is more
surreal than anything I've seen or heard back there.

An Aerial View of Wheatlands in Mid Autumn

'Indeed, it is a question if the exclusive reign of this
orthodox beauty is not approaching its last quarter.'
THOMAS HARDY, *The Return of the Native*

In the reciprocity of summer
And the year's first frosts, the green eruption
Hesitant, the stramineous remainder
Of last season's crop converts to nitrogen
As slowly overhead the spotter plane
Dissects the quickening flesh of Wheatlands,
The probing eye of the camera hidden
From your curious surveillance, while stands
Of mallee gnaw at the salty badlands.

They will offer to sell you the stolen
Moment, the frozen minutiae of your
Movement within the tableau, the tension
Extracted with such unwanted exposure:
The screams of the cockatoo, the tractor
Aching deep in its gut having swallowed
A brace of teeth as it crunched into gear,
Bleats of sheep on their way to be slaughtered,
The drift as a neighbour sprays weedicide.

Remember though that if given the chance
You would scrutinise someone else's yard,
So it may be worth adjusting your stance
In the light of such a double standard.
Forget that the land looks scarred and tortured:
That call for order in the rural scene,
For Virgil's countryside satiated
With weighty corn and Campanian wine,
And consumed by olives and wealthy swine,

Is not the harmony of this decade.
Instead look to the flux of soil and fire,
The low loping flight of the darkest bird,
The frantic dash of the land-bound plover,
The breaking of salt by errant samphire,
The flow of water after steady rain,
The everlasting in bright disorder,
The stealthy path of the predating plane
Cutting boundaries as you sow your grain.

First Eclogue

(for Frank Kermode)

GEOFF

> Got a moment, Steve? I need a hand tarping
> the field bin, the twenty-eights have just about
> finished levelling it off. They've had their feed.

STEVE

> Sure, I was wondering when you'd get to it –
> I've been sitting on the back verandah
> watching them rippling over the grain;
> most farmers would have taken to them
> with a shotgun, conscious of their pockets.

GEOFF

> And what, pollute their wheat with lead? Hardly
> worth it. No, every year I slightly
> overfill the bins, and let them at it.
> A kind of offering I guess. I'm just grateful
> that the place has been good to me these recent
> years. As you know, my old man struggled
> with drought and flood for a dozen years
> before I took over – it's been abundant
> since then. But still, I can't afford to let
> them have much more so I'd appreciate a hand!

STEVE

> I've been thinking about that well going salt
> down by the hundred acres, I reckon
> it's time you put in a few more trees,
> it's all very well thanking your lucky stars
> that things have gone so well, but keep in mind
> that fortune can turn at any time, at least
> if you don't try to keep one step ahead.
> Keep an eye out for the signs is my motto!

GEOFF

Yeah, I've been thinking much the same. Now,
if you'll climb up and toss those ropes
down to me, we'll get this tarp secured.
The air's a little unsteady as you'll have noticed,
and I don't want to be caught out by a summer storm.
Now, that's keeping an eye on the signs!

STEVE

Okay, I've secured this side. It would take
a cyclone to move it. Come on up
to the house for a drink. You might like
to see how I've done it up since we signed
that rental agreement. And put in a garden.

GEOFF

Well, since this is the last paddock, and once
I've delivered this load to the terminal
tomorrow morning, I can declare the harvest
finished, I'll take you up on that. How about
reciting one of those poems you're so fond of?

STEVE

A pleasure – nothing goes better with a beer.
We can sit on the verandah with our feet up,
watching as the atmosphere struggles above
the stubble, the birds now absent and a hollow
sound filling the emptiness. About
as far away from Perth as you can get.

GEOFF

Yes, I haven't had a chance to ask you how it went.
You went there to see your brother I think you said?
To tie up an estate after your father's death?

STEVE

That's true. But in many ways it seems
as if I never left the district.
That poem you asked for will double
as a description of my journey – I'll take
the verse that plays against the spirit of the City:

The city folk go to and fro
Behind a prison's bars,
They never feel the breezes blow
And never see the stars;
They never hear in blossomed trees
The music low and sweet
Of wild birds making melodies,
Nor catch the little laughing breeze
That whispers in the wheat.

That's from our Australian bard – Banjo
Paterson. Though over here in the West
we might see him as a foreigner,
he speaks a language closer to our own
than, say, the author of this old song:

The black-bird and the Thrush,
that made the woods to ring:
With all the rest, are now at hush,
and not a noate they sing.

GEOFF

Though if you changed the names of the birds
that last song could almost belong here.

STEVE

Yeah, I suppose you're right. Shit, I'm sweating like a pig.

GEOFF

It'll break soon. I reckon we're about
to get a heavy blow, if the red and black
of the sky are anything to go by; so I might
down this beer and head home before it hits.
Keep an eye out for lightning strikes. I pity
those who haven't finished getting their harvest in.

Second Eclogue

(PAUL *is delivering a load of grain to the local wheat bin. He is
at the weighbridge, talking with* JENNY, *the weighbridge officer.*)

PAUL

This load will be slightly under, the cops are up the road –
last year I went for a pile – they don't give you a break!
Is that a new guy down there on the grid?
Have they taken on an extra hand or are they replacing
someone who didn't pull his weight? Looks Chinese to me.
Gee, they've got half the world working in this place.

JENNY

Yeah, and the weighbridge officer's a girl! What's the world
coming to, eh? Soon it'll start affecting the yield.

PAUL

Eh, steady on, there's no need to be like that. I was
just making an observation. I know there's some people
around here that like things to remain the same, to not
let others in, but I've always said, give a bloke a go.
And a sheila too, for that matter! After all, we're pretty
lucky when you consider that this was once somebody
else's country. We've got to make room for others,
and respect the rights of those that came before us.
It's a bit of a balancing act, but better than being
at each other's throats. All I care about is that when people
look after their patch of ground they remember they
have neighbours. Mind you, all my mates say
I talk too much, and reckon I should get a soapbox
and set up in Supreme Court Gardens. But I never
go down to the city – I've enough trouble keeping up
with what's going on in the district. It's been a good
season though – give me a drought and I'd
be complaining. It'll be a magical sunset.

JENNY

What I love about it here, and I'm from the city,
is the distance between horizons. It's as if anything
is possible. The other day I was sitting in the shade
                down by the A-type bin, listening to the parrots
laughing as they feasted on spilt grain. For a moment
it was as if I could understand their language.
And though I can't recount what it was they said,
        I'm sure they made me welcome,
that they accepted me amongst them. Though I don't mind
saying, I can barely stand the heat. There's been some
talk of storms later in the week, that it's brewing up
                that way – it'll be a welcome relief! The ground
        seems as if it's gasping for a drink.

PAUL

Yeah, I agree, it's been a stinking week, but a storm can
wreck the harvest. Apart from damage to the crops
by wind and rain, there's always lightning ready
                to spark the tinder fields. Most years I've had
to drive my water truck out to a neighbour's place
and take to the flames with wet hessian. I've been lucky,
        the lightning's avoided my spread – touch wood!

JENNY

Well, I suppose you're right. Maybe I'll just sit back
with a nice cool drink this evening and think about
Antarctica. Though it'll be hard, as conversation
        gets heated in the hut after work.
The blokes find it annoying having a girl – a sheila! –
living amongst them. What's worse, they're two to a room
and I have a room to myself. Though I point out that I'd prefer
        the odds were stacked the other way!
But don't frown so much, they're not a bad bunch.
Just take getting used to, or a skin thicker than cow hide!
I'd like to yarn with you all day, but if we don't get
        this truck moving through to the grid
they'll be at me for slacking off. Enjoy the sunset!

PAUL

Thanks for that. And you're right, I'd better get a move on –
some other trucks have just rolled up to the sampling stand
and will be on your doorstep soon. Though I'll leave you
with lines from a song that's long been dear to me:

When the harvest sun sinks low,
And shadows stretch on the plain,
The roaring strippers come and go
Like ships on a sea of grain.

Firebreak

Out of the churned topsoil the bristles
of stubble tweak, the forest's tendrils
also stretch, but it's not the undergrowth

reaching out but veins snaking their way
out of the throat, the blast in its gasping
blowtorch breath blazing out, hurdling

the roads that surrounds the crops, that glow
like magnesium ribbon. Where the old and new meet
demarcation is no longer decipherable, unless it be

where farmers lay no fertiliser, the trash of low-grade
soil where protea and blackbutt, or york or salmon gum
further up the road grow against the odds,

dry and stark against the possibility of the lush
tableaux in which they are pocketed going up
in a rush, the firebans ignored as a spark leaps

from the comb hitting a cairn or a scratch
of quartz, the magnetic contraction, scintillating the threat
to a fire truck bogged to the axles, as if to say

don't come closer, this is consecrated earth, or the brown
frame a survey line, a picket against insurance
assessments and controlled burns

or where the suburb meets the bush, the black-grey sand
like a stygian creek lobbing its way nowhere, its banks
weedy and choked with cape tulip, hot pink against

the uncomfortable bush that invades, a white plaster cupid
with its wings snapped off and face stuck in the dirt,
arse sticking skywards not as an act of defiance

but of utter defeat – not by the bush
but the implication that a fresh cupid
will stand on the soles of its feet

that in a pine forest just off a firebreak
some guy had built a bunker in which to imprison
and then kill his family – *cordon sanitaire*

where the darkness stirs and everything below the pine
needles is dead and the firebreaks move like congealing
blood, thicker than the fire trails of conscience,

as if the fire's supposed to take time out and hesitate
while firefighters hit back, staunching the flow,
or surrounding it, or bombing it from the air

the breathless air where language
implicates itself in gasps – Heraclitus
says that you can't step into the same river twice

so the dried-up waterbed is proof of damming
and irrigation upstream charts a wasteland
further downstream

that if you don't tend to your firebreaks
you'll be in strife with the council whose inspectors
ARE always on the move, at least if you watch them

through a farmer's field glasses, the plover rising
quickly over the tinder-dry crops, machinery brooding
like humidity on the fringes

the paddy melons bursting at the seams,
or *in flagrante delicto*, their comeuppance
in the bindy bindies crawling, scratching

you can't afford to be smart when it comes to firebreaks,
flames eat wit, and when fire has stopped on the thin line
the heat-drawn foliage chills, ash on the ploughed ground

dugite skin enjambed in the fork of a dead limb
fallen across the bend, linking crop to crop
fuelling recollection in the flash of firestorm

though it's not like having the fire against the ropes
because the only rules it recognises are those of nature,
it's natural justice to behave *absurdum dicta*

as one has a right to do, hidden clauses in dubious contracts
drawn up by profiteers and interpreted by caricatures
with low self-opinions who see themselves as mercurial

firebrands – inspired and thorough in the execution
of their responsibilities, or on the flipside, those who
think it poetic to ignore or even spread disinformation

about fire bans, who think comfort's a great lark
and only those quick enough will enjoy its fruits
lest their lushness is flurried in the vacuum

others being quick to dob someone in as diversion, like a witch
trial in the cauldron of summer, tempers short and the pub
exploding nightly, the cops with their scales looking

for excess as truckies thunder towards the bins, themselves
surrounded by firebreaks, and firebreaks siding the roads
all the way in – aggro means ignition –

that maybe on one side of the break creatures
with souls existed while on the other the machine organisms
of Descartian soullessness moved on (liminal) limbs

so, when firebreaks were cut by horse-drawn ploughs,
huge draught horses champing against the bit,
damp hessian smoked like a European victory.

Corrugations

(for Paul Kane)

Hovering on the liquid chassis,
Gyroscopic and pneumatic, bold
In the almost equal and opposite reaction,
A steady future in which the leaves
Don't arrange themselves haphazardly –
The reading a fact, and the driver
Arrogantly confident, teeth busy
With a wad of gum, working
The digestive juices on a long country road,
Passing cool houses with federation verandahs,
Or scant shacks with the sun cutting
Back like smashed glass off the zinc peaks
Of corrugated iron, or, conversely,
Wallowing in the rusted troughs,
Ambient in the mythology of the battler,
As the thin branch of a spotted gum
Dropped by a strong hot blast
Cracks insipidly beneath the tyres
Of a well-shod carriage that'll level out
Unevenness or indiscretion – parody
Of the bone rattlers that headed this way
During the gold rush sunk with water –
Until all smoothness is ironed out
Of the slick market economy,
And a flipside of a song of origin
Severs the lashing tongue of bitumen,
A black recollection in the rear-vision mirror
As the corrugation in the truck-shattered
Gravel bites back, jarring the car's architecture
And confidence, ricocheting a shakedown
Exploding with mimicry, blurring
The harsh if picturesque backdrop.

Mementoes

They're scanning the farm
with camera and video
and scribbling notes
like ragged scrub
into exercise books –
words and images
tearing at the flesh
like a scourge.
There seems so much
to take away, to preserve
in what has always
been a casual family
archive. The temptation
to invoke flood and drought
along with seasons
of almost gratuitous
fertility, to take
blood-brown loam
or salt crystals
from lowland –
where the richness
over the decades
has come undone –
almost overwhelms them.
Not that they speak
this out loud,
but they think it,
and know they'll say
later that it's what
they should have done,
when they had
the chance – this new home
a world away.

The Journey

There was nothing else to do
but position the corpse
in the cabin – the back
of the ute
full of fencing gear
which his father
wasn't about to leave
out in the middle
of nowhere.
So he had to sit
in between like an apostrophe –
as if holding the soul
to the body.
'He's still pretty fresh –
I'd hazard a guess
that his heart packed
it in. What he was
doing out there
Hell only knows!
Waterless, and the sun furious!'
bellowed his father.
So he sat there as the corpse
stiffened, held to the seat
by the belt. He didn't look at it
once during the journey,
though could sense
the anger in his father
at having to go so far out of their way –
his thick sweat poisonous
as the ute
eroded those miles
into town.

The Whistle

We thought him
a musician we could
cope with – a Pied Piper
who belonged to the place –
going out there with his whistle
and calling the foxes,
bringing in the skins
and collecting the bounties;
sometimes we stroked the red
bodies, looked into their eyes,
examined the needle-sharp teeth –
'Don't prick yourself on those things,'
he'd say, 'never know what they
might carry.' And we'd grin,
though moving our hands
sharply away. He had us hooked.
We begged to hear him whistle
up a tune, but he denied us.
Our parents told us
to leave him alone, he had
a job to do and shouldn't be
distracted. As we grew older
we heard stories about him.
And the foxes were hunted out.
We defended him, though
with queasy stomachs.
None of us owning guns
and all of us realising
we'd heard without knowing
the strains of the whistle.

The Trap
(for George Steiner)

The district was being broken up into small
lots and weekend farmers were buying up. Hatfield
     bought a hundred hectares
     of premium land. Not
short of a dollar, he set out to create the
perfect farm, working from the ground up – importing

a top-of-the-range kit home, mains power, computer,
massive concrete water tanks. He had the fencers
     hard at work ensuring
     nothing got in or out.
He stocked the place with a flock of stud merinos,
setting himself up instantly as a breeder
     of note. A few thoroughbred
horses and an artificial lake crowned his State.

A city psychiatrist in private practice
he easily managed his appointment book such
     that he could get up to
     his spread regularly.
He hired a manager who drove out from town
daily, to check things were running smoothly. But one
     thing gnawed at him deeply –
the rank old fellow who owned the place next door ran

a dismal show, an embarrassment that wouldn't
go away. And despite his manager's constant
     assurances, he was
     convinced that disease would
cross his borders and infect his flock, that patches
of salt would creep up under his bristling fences
     and catch him in his sleep.
To make things worse, the old fellow muttered under

his breath and couldn't be understood. 'Just listen
closely,' his manager said, 'he's been here all his
life and knows everything
there is to know about
farming.' But from the look Hatfield shot him he knew
not to bring the subject up again. 'I'll buy him out!'
Hatfield said to a friend.
'A thousand hectares is more than I need but I'm

sure I'll get approval to break it up and might
even turn a profit.' His advances were laughed
off. When his children came
to stay for holidays
he warned them to keep away from the Cesspit as
he'd come to call it; first chance, they tackled the fence,
tearing trousers and shirts,
and wandered into the rocky scrub, explored the

salt flats and gulleys. Sometimes they saw *him* in the
distance, though he didn't seem to care that they were
there. The Cesspit was rife
with bird life – the plover,
the blue heron, rosellas and twenty-eights, crows,
sulphur-crested cockatoos, and zebra finches –
and they lamented that
their father's place was green but dead. Even the lake

seemed too blue. The Cesspit's dams were rippled and cragged
and the water a murky brown; old windmills snarled
their mangled hands but turned
steadily 'round, even when
the wind was barely a whisper. The sheep seemed wild
and some still had their tails. But the fodder was thick
and diverse, and it was
as if the sheep belonged to this bizarre landscape.

At the dinner table their father would warn them
off, threatening the city for the remainder
of their school holidays.
'You can't trust these inbreeds.'
They wondered what he meant, and also when he said
to the manager, 'The sun has charred him to the
bone' or 'he's got a touch
of the tar.' The manager laughed uncomfortably.

One night they took a torch and scaled the fence, hoping
to spot owls, bats or maybe a tawny frogmouth.
      A rabbit sat transfixed
      by the torch beam before
launching suddenly into the undergrowth. Though
wearing only sandshoes and conscious of snakes, they
      plunged into the pooling
darkness. In the dry air they could smell eucalypt

and the freshly upturned earth of rabbit diggings.
They approached the warrens and then one of them screamed
      'It's got my foot! It's got
      my foot!' She almost passed
out with the pain as her brother struggled to prise
open the jaws of the trap, its rust-red teeth deep
    into the shoe and flesh,
brown earth clotting in lumps. Freed, she struggled on her

brother's arm towards the fence, the torchlight crazy
against the night. Their father was at the back door
      as they approached, having
      heard the scream. 'I'll have the
bastard strung up from one of his own trees!' he yelled
as the boy tried to explain. His children safe in
      the city, he approached
the law who said there was nothing they could do as

it was private property and the kids shouldn't
have been there. Normally a sober man, Hatfield
      polished off a bottle
      of whiskey late one night,
took a drum of petrol, climbed his state-of-the-art
fence, and brought fire to the pit of his hatred.

Paddy Melons

Our uncle recalls our
popping paddy melons
as clearly as he remembers
gates being left open –

both acts of pollution,
upsetting good husbandry –
seeds dispersed over
freshly ploughed fields,

sheep wandering
into thick crops, getting
into the harvested grain,
found swollen and near death

on the banks of the dam.
That it reminded us
of bursting the cells
of bubble wrap

is residual
in my memory;
while in his it persists
like a notch carved

through a rough surface
the consistency of bark,
deep into the rings
of adversity.

Pig Melons

As children we dashed
their brains out,
the insipid flesh
drying like chunks of pork
over the yellowing paddocks;
this murder bringing
further ruin to arable lands,
choking the native flora
with spilt thoughts
encoded as seeds
that bided their time
spitefully
until the rains
washed away the tracks
of our games, our conflicts,
percolating beneath the surface,
throwing ropes
that crept out,
securing the meagre
fertility of the place
with their rituals
of bondage.

Courtship and Country Towns

(for Elizabeth Riddell)

Without really knowing why,
they found themselves
getting away to the city
or neighbouring towns

whenever the opportunity
arose. It wasn't that they
disliked the girls they'd
grown up with, rather

that they were almost sisters
and it seemed a little strange
setting up for life with family.
Sure, it was okay messing

around behind the woodshed,
or on the school bus, or after
a bottle of green ginger wine
at a dance, but these were things

you did with no strings
attached. And the girls
seemed to prefer blokes
visiting from the city,

or the neighbouring district.
Their mums all said it's a pity,
it would be nice to see our
families wed, but the wind

disperses the seeds of a dandelion
so that they spread and find room
to prosper in fertile earth.
This town has a constant

thirst for new blood,
despite the papers claiming
it's slowly dying, and, in any case,
dandelions were introduced.

Waterbag

The heat warping
eyesight and rising
in shimmers over stubble
already charred to the ground,
the temperature
in the waterbag
drops – slung beneath
a cold-blooded wandoo
searing air rips
moisture from its pulpy skin,
rapid evaporation
inducing such a chill
at the core
of the canvas goitre
that the world
is turned
upside down.

Death of a Farm Boy

Rebelliously
leaning his rifle
against the taut wires
of the fence
he stepped over,
pivoting
on his leading foot
watching as the barrel
began its slow arc
towards him;
the hair trigger
jarring
as the bead
of the sights
clipped a barbed twist,
the crack of firing
annihilating
the quail-heavy
fields.

The Widower's Daughter

A picture of health
she glowed like the best crops
of a fine year, golden red
with sunset, almost
phosphorescent when the warm
slow evenings nuzzled
towards harvest.
And strong with it,
quick to behead a dugite
creeping up
through the rockery
and onto the verandah.
'Lopped it with the shovel!'
he'd brag.
Couldn't recognise it.
Not a piece left bigger
than a finger. The venom
crushed out of its head.
'She's a healthy specimen
for sure!' he'd say...
the clean air,
fertile country,
a doting father
to keep her company.

Hammock

The kids found him
floating in the hammock,
swinging slowly
beneath the back verandah
with the evening breeze –
big as a cow, they reckoned.
Sure enough, he'd blown up
to three times his size,
and he'd been big
to start with.
The air smelt
like the pig shed,
not that they noticed
the stench.
It looked too strange
for them to be horrified.
Rather they stared for an age
before coming to find me
cursing the mess
in the kitchen.

The Rearing Tractor

It was as if the wild
had got hold of it –
'the old girl' –
as if the careful
tune-up had reinvigorated,
had given bite –
and as it reared
those around got
caught up
in the irrepressibly
slow take of it,
like the bomber pilot
in Dr Strangelove
riding the nuclear bomb down
over the USSR,
going down swinging,
watching on
as if it were
the thing to do
as he lay crushed
beneath its cumbersome
bulk, the wheels
still turning,
its gender
a talking point.

The Fall

In the flatlands
children make empires
out of lone trees
or an aerial rising
high above the house –
a lightning strike
stretched to remove the kinks
and set as a totem
to the static of isolation.
They'd always called
him a wild boy
with his unkempt
shock of red hair;
a fireball crashing
through the atmosphere
from a forbidden perch
up high, a plunge
by which an onlooker
could only have made
the darkest of wishes.

Warren

His name
was really Warren,
that rabbiter
with the bad leg –
the pain that made him bitter,
that drove him cursing
out onto the Nullarbor,
stocked up with liquor,
ammunition, his dogs.
That drove him into the place
where space was the inside
of a tin humpy, and not
the outside world
which was an endless field
resisting definition,
where focus
was the sharp line
of the horizon, the wicked
teeth of traps,
the breath held
in the moment
he squeezed the trigger.

The Rabbiters: A Pastoral

(for Douglas Barbour)

That the Theocritan ute has been versed
in country things seems obvious, the velour
on the dashboard crazy with fresh air
rushing through the doorless cabin, the cursed
skies blackened by night. Though a moon lurks
somewhere and the spotlight cutting through
the burn-back of summer detects the jerks
of nerves and tissue – the rabbits out to chew
the burnt prongs of stubble, the halogen's
conflagration filling the omni-screens
within their eyeballs – the crack and whine
of a triple two mocks its rituals, a sign
of fading influence in a field where gravity
is a neck chop and the poem is framed by levity.

Mange

He'd shoot though
wouldn't touch them –
skinning only the lustrous ones,
leaving those affected
to rot where they dropped.
And even though
he never came into contact
with skin eaten
and fur dropping in clots
he'd still feel the mange
get under his covering,
his skin itching
like it did
when the barber
gave him a trim.

Terraforming
(for Jeremy)

A prey bird flies
    suddenly
cedilla in its grasp
with carrion anonymity,
thwarting pacts and boundaries
as cold fronts and accrued
    ordinance
encrypt with rumour;
the ruffled field a plough's scamming
profit in scannable lines of sowing,
    as legend or grand design,
pinpointing a subject,
    having the presence of mind,
the evolutionary
          tact to ignore
the glowing reports of order.

The Elusive Night Heron

The elusive night heron
With the weight of the old world
On its hunched shoulders
Roosting primeval during
The bright light of day
Will prowl the swamps
With evening's closure,
Its ethereal visitation
Doubly camouflaged & reinforced
Like stealth. Sometimes
Out rabbit shooting they'll
Catch it in the spotlight –
Set like wood it dares them
To lay down their guns
And return the night
To its silent hunters.

The Visitation

Old timers reckon they've seen it before
but others have their doubts, that rabbit virus
got loose not long before the roos were
struck down blind – crashing into fences,
drowning in dams, insane in the forests.
As they examine the scene of this disaster
the skull of a fox grins among the ashes
as if it should be there, totemic welcome,
an irony of invasion and predation.
The fire circles like some extraterrestrial
sign-posting, landing or communication
points, heat's corolla a beacon. Everyone
there has experienced something unusual
at one time or another. As children, their fathers
drove wildly to escape the tracking light.
At night they'd watch the fields glow,
or the hills silhouetted against the darkness.
The odd telegraph insulator brightens
the picture, but with the end of winter
the dullness returns. Train lines
lead into the green of a paddock,
submerged in the sodden crop
on the forest's edge. Swathes of she-oaks
mimic the wind, doubling its intensity,
like amplifiers. The scene breaks up.
Caught mid-leap – prehistoric – decay
an aesthetic within the dried-skin bandage.
Dead kangaroos see deep below
the surface like infernal visitors.
Who can read and translate these signs?
Who can read the blind leap into the arms
of history, a serial killer armed with a shotgun
and dressed up as a farmer or forest ranger?
A white-faced heron prods a blown carcass
as if it were a body of water, organs rippling
round a petrified spine, tides moving
counter-clockwise in the brittle skull.
The harmonics of the forest approach
a pure tone, an incestuous object hovering
dangerously over the many corpses.

On the Transferring of Three Generations of Family Ashes from their Graves – A Farewell to Wheatlands
(for Lorraine Wheeler)

And the ashes will be lifted out of the loam
and carried to the foot of Mount Bakewell,
lifted out of the mummified flesh
of the farm, to await their new shape,
farm-bones showing through parched skin
scratched up by the random though determined
assaults of wind-flurries upside-downing
the ordnance, usurping maps
with strain and nervous tension,
harassing the labourers shovelling grain,
grimacing about the gargoyle-spouts of the silos
working on regardless, as if there's
something to this bullshit about 'cycles',
as if the repetition of drive-belts
and insistent circuits of pink and grey galahs
raucous over the Aztec accumulations
of mudbrick are *de rigueur,* as if this grave-plot
within its aging fence IS the New World,
as if last year's harrowed ground
blackens round the rim like the fire-gutted
home of a family that left a long way back
because they'd no choice, because terraces
of termites are inevitable, their forms
rising and falling in the weirding grasses,
yellow in the thin waves of tainted summer,
each grave noted as a milestone
on the road to repetition, anonymity.
And the ashes will be lifted out of the loam
and carried to the foot of Mount Bakewell.

Each year Paterson's Curse decorates the farm
like kitsch – even during this savage dry
which must break soon. That in rich soil
mechanisms of purple flowers
drive to draw sunlight
to its awl, this weed that would

consume the fields, a cover-all
that plasters wounds inflicted
by ball & chain, the stain
that is the sun's unreturnable gift,
plovers charging burnished bones
of liveried beasts fallen in heaps
with the limitless summer.
And the ashes will be lifted out of the loam
and carried to the foot of Mount Bakewell.

Rose quartz sparkles about
a wandoo altar, a dugite's skin
mimicking the detritus of woodpiles
as the new owners check out the place
and wonder where it is they stand.
When the family first arrived they
reckoned it was theirs for the taking.
A gift from God. The shadows
were driven back into the trees,
where it was guessed they belonged.
And now the wide open fields
are both shadowless and treeless.
The place's name has been lost.
The territory remains
but with boundaries redrawn.
Later, they'll embrace beneath a tree
none of you had noticed before
and it will become *their* sacred place,
and be named accordingly.
And the ashes will be lifted out of the loam
and carried to the foot of Mount Bakewell.

A patch of fallen grain
lifts light in varicoloured
paddocks; and the people of the district,
for all their apparent crimes,
will get rid of you before
you get rid of them, and the smaller
their spread, their tractor, the truck
they've used for carting grain,
the more they'll remain and prosper.
And the ashes will be lifted out of the loam
and carried to the foot of Mount Bakewell.

The sun burns its wealth
into your skin until
you can't take any more
and stay indoors. Though
like all finite resources it pullulates
about the steady state
of your faith – but you can't
afford to drop the price
despite the state of fences and firebreaks
around the dams and gulleys.
And the ashes will be lifted out of the loam
and carried to the foot of Mount Bakewell.

And the old chev truck that's sat
fixed like sculpture for thirty years
moves indiscernibly as a black-faced
cuckoo shrike twirls in a pepper tree,
or darts from machinery in the new shed
down to the river gums at the neck
of the salt, and old wells breathe
through cracks in railway sleepers
or rusty sheets of corrugated iron.
The arteries beneath the farm
are indifferent to the polypipe's
black mimicry, the pseudo songlines
of a temporary occupation.
And the ashes will be lifted out of the loam
and carried to the foot of Mount Bakewell.

The family has gathered for Christmas
and while the younger cousins
that you spent your childhood with
clarify memory and *your* having been there,
the oldest cousin whose life
had little to do with yours
expresses surprise at your recall.
It is as if you were never part of it.
You point out that *he* hadn't 'been there' –
an older boy ignoring the 'kids'.
He's astonished when you remember
Gerry milking Princess the cow,
and that his horse Treasure,

frenzied by a lightning strike,
was found dead, hooked in a forked tree.
And he talks of the stubble being burnt –
strange ritual with his father
as master of the ceremony –
flames burning towards the centre,
eating each other's breath,
leaving the paddock black and indelible
and hungry for seed and nutrients.
And the ashes will be lifted out of the loam
and carried to the foot of Mount Bakewell.

The Doppler Effect and the Australian Pastoral

Red Shift

In memory it moves steadily into the red
as if the feathers of a Western Rosella
are blood, and time is the application
of heat to the seen, the fox moving with the rapid
beat of lightning coruscating the vermilion rim
of a constant daybreak or nightfall, dry thunder the applause
of a crowd crazy about the exits, as if towns squat
close to the sparking dirt, or dissemble into their
constituents through prisms of salt crystals,
and all of it moving away from you like
the fading drone of the water truck,
the receding dams, the shed skins
of black polythene pipe growing brittle
like the black expanse of an expanding universe
captured and defined, its escape realised,
plotted and planned, the bird traps set
on the periphery of the farm,
the increasingly rare birds
perishing as the property
changes hands and the hunters
forget to disarm the drought.

Blue Shift

The rich blood of action
coming through like a bullet,
all birds with blue feathers
squawking at the top of their voices

as if the deeply blue sky
is the centre and all is thundering
towards it, the desolate expanse
a ruse, feigning infertility –

drought the cranky codger
who is at once a brown snake
and a racehorse goanna, or the creek
heavy with night, grotesque

and bristling with myth –
as if it's always been almost upon us
and we're just beginning to see
beyond the construct of history.

The Machine of the Twentieth Century Rolls Through the High-Yielding Crop

Dust particles cling to sweat despite the sun just up,
moisture levels within brittle stalks drop
as rapidly as markets are lost or gained, shadow
puppetry of information exchange leading the finest
of mechanical technologies astray, as over the crop

the machine of the twentieth century poises – straining
against dry dock, a Titanic that won't be sunk in those deepest
spots of abundance, a post-modern Ceres busy at the helm
lest a hidden rock break the fingers clawing in the grain;
this schizophrenic God whose speech is a rustle, a token bristling

like static on the stereo, despite state-of-the-art electronics
and a bathyspherical cabin of glass and plastic sealed
against all intrusion though retaining hawk-like vision and radio
contact with the outside world. On the fringes – at home base,
or by the gate – the workers are ready to launch out, to drain

grain from a bulging bin. The art of harvesting is in the hiding
of the operation. Behind clean lines and sun-deflecting paint
the guts of the machine work furiously; from point of entry
to expulsion the process is relentless – from comb working greedily,
grain spirals up elevators, thrashed in a drum

at tremendous speeds, straw spewed out back by
manic straw-walkers, the kernels falling to sieves below
as fans drive cocky chaff out into the viscous
daylight. The sun at mid-morning rages out of control,
glutted on this excess fuel. Melanomas spread on field workers

as they tarp a load; the driver plunges with precision
back into the crop, setting a perfect line, de-mystifying
this inland sea – an illusion, a mirage that hangs around
just before summer has reached full-blown. City granaries
filling, factories churning, 'design' a catchword instigating

plenty – the risks of intensive farming, tomorrow's worry –
stubble itching, high yields floating like oil on troubled waters,
the Titanic's myth attracting the districts of the hungry.

Dematerialising the Poisoned Pastoral

With the time lapse, the upturned echidna writhes,
    ants and maggots consuming its sponge-like
    flesh beneath the spreading International Klein Blue sky –
just a component part of an heroic *Blaues Schwammrelief* –
the residue of its life flashing by, as sun-eaten locals
    stare uncomprehendingly at the skins of their

finest sheep strung out over rusty fences, all veined
    and varicosed with ordnance despite
    tableaux of monochromatic sameness,
as if each were a small centre, a source of density –
the sky, the dam water, the raddled paddocks and graded roads,
    those soft diggings around fallen trees multiplying

each night, writ in mystical latin: *Tachyglossus aculeatus*.
    Beneath the picture subterranean streams overflow,
    underwriting patches of poison bush that'd see
the whole flock stone dead on the spread, blue as blue Venus
in a deeply blue light, blue as the International Klein Blue sea
    beside which the locals spend their holidays.

John Kinsella was born in Perth, Western Australia, in 1963. He studied at The University of Western Australia and travelled extensively for a number of years through Europe, the Middle East, and Asia. After returning to Western Australia he lived in various suburban and rural areas and had various jobs. He is the founding editor of the international poetry magazine *Salt*. He now lives in Cambridge and divides his time between Britain and Australia; he is a By-Fellow of Churchill College.

John Kinsella has published poems in a large number of literary journals in Australia, the USA, Britain, New Zealand, Japan, India and Canada. He has published twelve collections of poetry in Australia, and four books in Britain: *The Silo* and *The Undertow: New & Selected Poems* from Arc, and *Poems 1980-1994* and *The Hunt and other poems* from Bloodaxe. His many prizes include the John Bray Award for Poetry from the Adelaide Festival.

He has given readings of his work in Britain, Ireland, the USA, Spain, France and Germany. He has received writing grants from both the Western Australian Department for the Arts and the Literature Board of the Australia Council. In 1996 he received a Young Australian Creative Fellowship and has recently been awarded a two-year Fellowship from the Literature Board of the Australia Council.